STICKER ATLAS
ZOO ANIMALS
OF THE WORLD

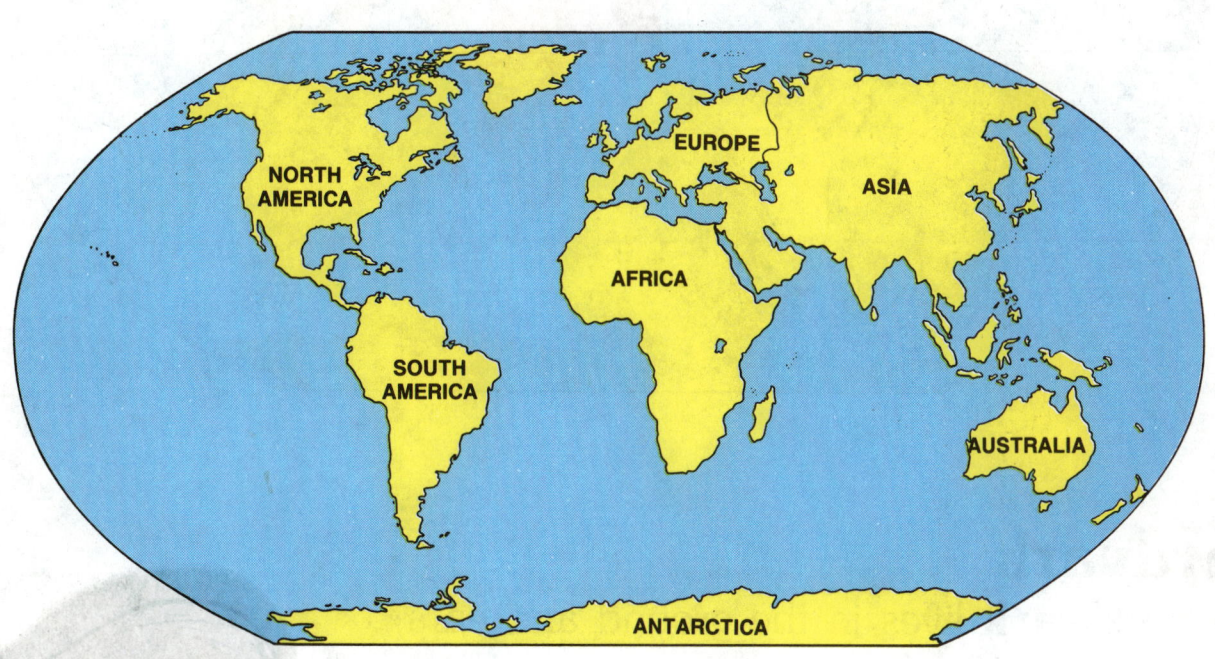

Cover and Interior Art
MJ Studios Inc.
Written by Carol Z. Bloch
M.Ed. The Johns Hopkins University
B.A. The George Washington University

Copyright © 1991 Nickel Press

AFRICA

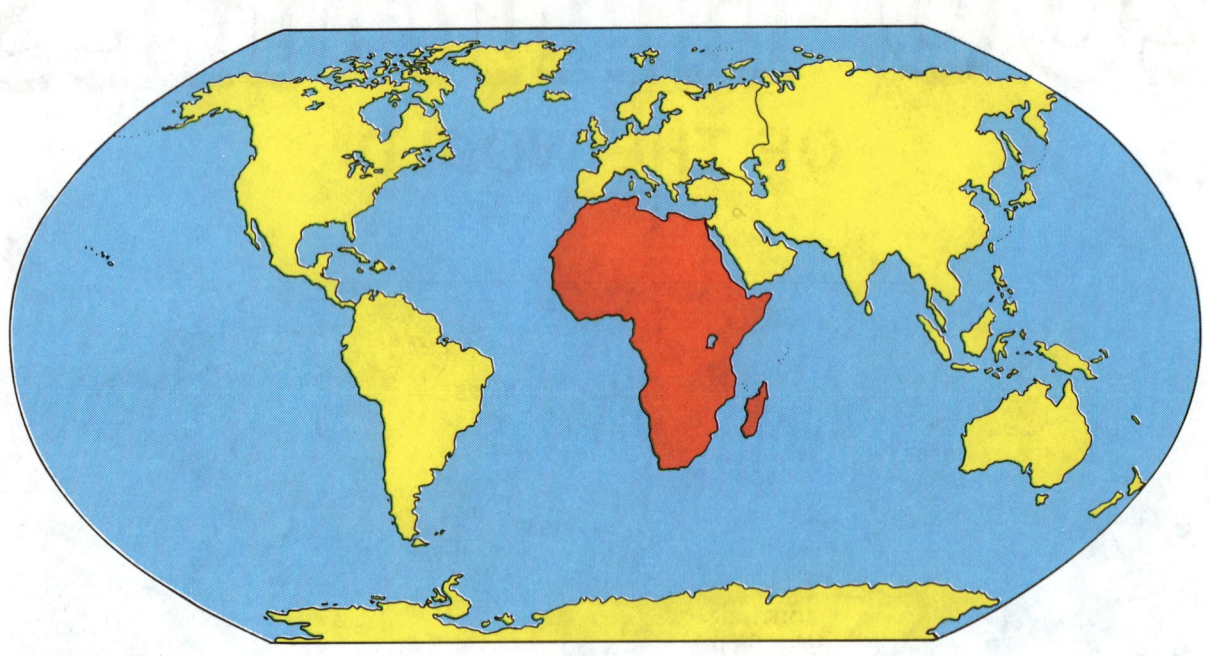

Aardvark
The **aardvark** lives in the ground and eats ants and termites. It has a long snout and a sticky tongue which it uses to catch insects. It sleeps all day and hunts for food at night. It uses its strong claws to dig and to defend itself.

Arabian Camel
The **arabian camel** or **dromedary** is a one humped camel with short hair. The hump is made up of fat that helps feed the animal when it cannot find food. This funny-looking animal can go without water for three to four days. It lives in the sandy desert feeding on grasses, leaves and dates.

Cheetah

The **cheetah** is the world's fastest animal on land. This beautiful member of the cat family is yellow with black spots covering its body. It is a quiet and shy animal that hunts in pairs or in a group. The **cheetah** lives in open grasslands living mainly on small animals.

Chimpanzee

The **chimpanzee** is a noisy, social and intelligent animal that is most like a human. A **chimp** lives in a large community where it shares fruit and grasses. It is covered with long black hair, has long arms and short legs and can walk upright for a short distance. It sleeps in the trees in the rainforest and communicates with others by making different kinds of sounds.

Elephant

The **elephant** is the largest land animal in the world. It can weigh as much as 14,000 pounds. Its nose is a long trunk which it uses as a hand and to carry food and water to its mouth. The **elephant's** tusks are actually huge teeth made of ivory. Herds, or groups of **elephants**, roam the jungles and plains in search of bark, leaves and fruit.

Gazelle

The **gazelle** is a slender, light brown antelope that is very graceful. It grows ringed horns that may be curved or straight. When it senses danger, it jumps straight up and down to signal to the others in the herd. It nibbles on grasses and plants in grassland areas.

Giant Eland

The **giant eland** is the largest living antelope. There are only a few dozen left in the world. Although it has a very heavy body, it can jump very high. Its horns can grow to almost four feet. It lives in the grasslands eating mostly leaves and grasses.

Giraffe

The **giraffe** is the world's tallest animal. It can grow to almost 18 feet in height. It uses this height to gather fruit and leaves to eat. Its yellow and brown coloring helps protect it by making it hard to see in the grassy areas in which it lives. The **giraffe** usually sleeps standing up.

Gorilla

The **gorilla** is the largest of all apes. Its body is covered with black or brown hair and it has very large teeth. It looks scary but is actually gentle and shy. When it wants to frighten others, it stands on its hind legs and beats on its chest. **Gorillas** live in the rainforest and travel in groups. They feed on leaves, bark and fruit, and wrestle with each other for fun.

Hippopotamus

The river **hippopotamus** is a very large animal that lives on land and in the water. It is a very good swimmer. Its skin is thick and brown and it has no hair. The smaller pygmy **hippopotamus** has blackish skin and lives in the forest near streams. They both eat fruit, vegetables and leaves.

Impala

The **impala** is the most plentiful of all African antelope. This graceful, reddish-brown animal jumps and leaps quickly to safety when danger is near. Males often fight by pushing at each other with their horns. The **impala** lives in grassy areas grazing on shrubs, herbs and grasses.

Jackal

A **jackal** is similar to a wolf. It signals the beginning and the end of its hunt by howling loudly. It may hunt alone or in a small pack. Its home is the grassy plains where it preys on sheep, gazelle and other animals. Its keen sense of smell helps it hunt for food.

Lion

The **lion** is probably the most famous member of the cat family. It is known as the "king of beasts" because of its beauty and strength. The male **lion** has a shaggy mane covering its head and large, sharp claws and teeth. It lives in the woodlands and grasslands and hunts other animals for food.

Ostrich

The **ostrich** is the largest living bird. This strange looking bird has wings but cannot fly. It is the fastest two legged creature on earth. Its incredible, long, elastic throat allows it to swallow objects as well as insects, seeds and grass. It lives in grasslands and semi-desert areas.

Ratel

The black and gray **ratel** is often called a **honey badger** because of its love of honey. Its thick coat and skin help prevent bee stings from hurting it. It also likes to eat insects and hunt for small animals. The **ratel** is at home in many environments from forests to grasslands.

Rhinoceros

The **rhinoceros** is one of the largest land animals in the world. It uses its nose horn to defend itself against enemies by charging at great speed. It cools off its thick skin by wallowing in the mud. A **rhino** likes to live alone in grassy areas and swamps, feeding on leaves and bark.

Sable Antelope

The **sable antelope** is large in size and has a shiny, black coat with white on its face and underside. Males have horns that curve backwards which can grow to 40 inches long. It lives in grassland areas and seeks out grasses and leaves to eat.

Spotted Hyena

The **spotted hyena** looks like a large, yellow-gray dog with dark spots. Its loud giggle and yell can be heard across the plains. The **hyena** is an excellent hunter that hunts in a pack with others for small animals and fruit. It is often called a "laughing hyena" because of the sound it makes after killing an animal.

Warthog

The **warthog** is one of the scariest-looking animals in the world. The male has a long, flat head with bumps on it. There are four tusks that stick out from the sides of its snout. It is actually a peaceful animal that will run from danger. A **warthog** likes to wallow in the mud and feeds on grasses.

Wildebeest

The **wildebeest** is also known as a **gnu** and is a member of the antelope family. It has a large head and thick horns, a stiff beard and a tail like a horse. Its grunt sounds like a frog. The **wildebeest** is always on the move in grassy areas and plains looking for water and grass.

Zebra

The **zebra** is a horse-like animal with black and white stripes. No two **zebras** have the same pattern of stripes. The **zebra** lives in a large herd where it may recognize other members of the herd by voice or stripe pattern. It grazes on short grass and leaves and is usually found near water in grasslands.

Zorilla

The **zorilla** is the world's smelliest creature. It has a thick black coat with white stripes and looks like a skunk. When frightened it will scream, lift its tail and spray its enemy with a smelly fluid. A **zorilla** lives alone roaming open grasslands. At night it searches for small animals, birds and snakes to eat.

ANTARCTICA

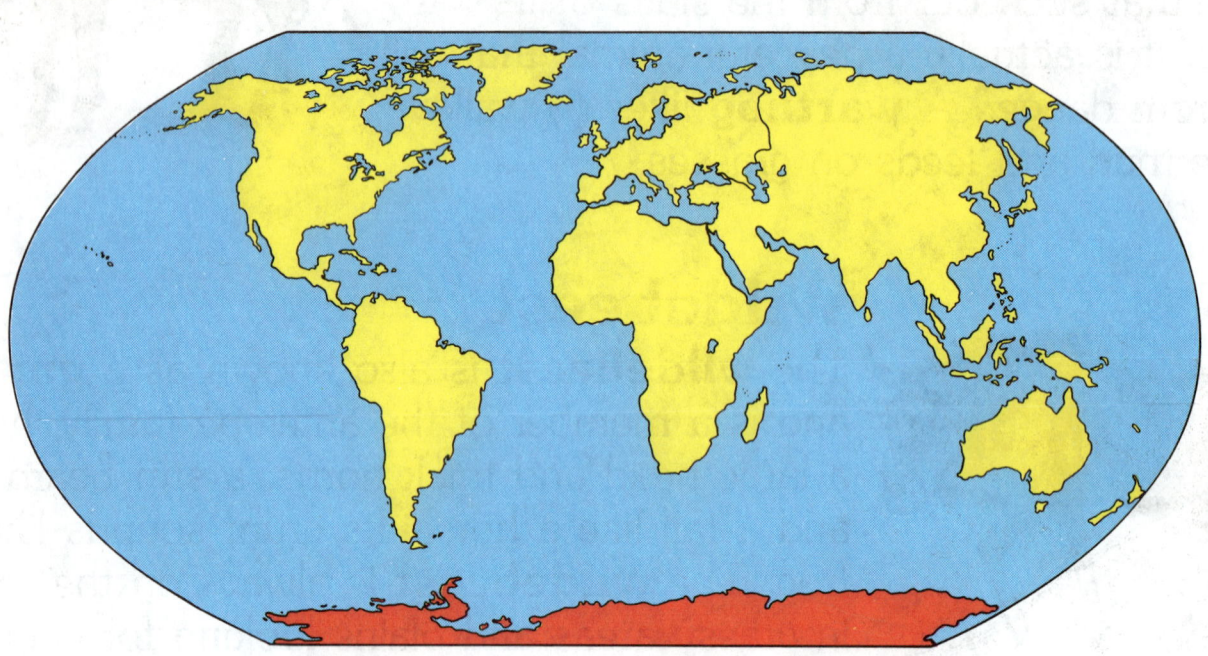

Albatross
The **albatross** is a beautiful, large sea bird. Its long, powerful bill catches fish and squid to eat. It also feeds on bits of food thrown from ships. The **albatross** glides high in the sky constantly searching for food.

Blue Whale
The **blue whale** is the largest animal in the world growing up to 100 feet long. It feeds only four or five months out of the year on small fish and "krill", a shrimp-like creature. Whales, unlike fish, have lungs and must come to the surface sometimes to breathe air.

Crabeater Seal

There are more than 30 million **crabeater seals** in the Antarctic region making it the most common mammal in the world. It is one of the fastest seals on ice and land. It feeds mainly on "krill", a small shrimp-like creature. All seals have paddle-like feet called flippers.

Leopard Seal

The **leopard seal** is the only animal that feeds on seals, penguins, and other animals. It has a graceful body, a large head and is covered with dark spots. The **leopard seal** is an excellent swimmer and has a thick layer of blubber that keeps it warm.

Penguin

The **penguin** is an unusual bird that cannot fly. It stands upright and waddles on its short legs. It is an excellent swimmer, catching fish for food. The largest **penguin** stands four feet tall. A **penguin** lives with many others in huge groups called "rookeries".

Southern Elephant Seal

The **southern elephant seal** is the world's largest seal. It is also known as a "sea elephant" and may weigh up to 8,000 pounds. It is named for its large nose and tough skin. This huge seal can stop eating for a long time, living off its blubber.

ASIA

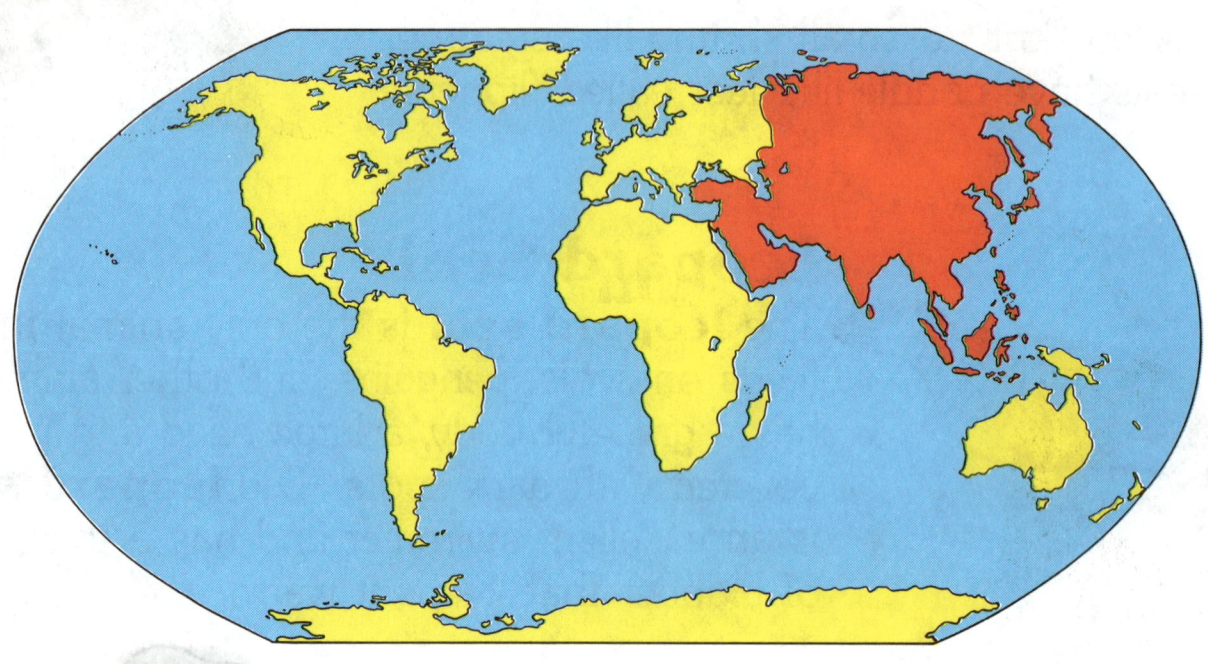

Binturong

The **binturong** is a rarely seen black, furry animal. It uses its strong, heavy tail as an extra hand as it moves from tree to tree. Its excellent sense of smell helps it hunt for small animals, birds and fruit. A **binturong** communicates with others by leaving a strong scent where it has been.

Gaur

The **gaur** has a dark brown coat with stocking-like white marks on its lower legs. It is the largest of all wild cattle. A **gaur** lives in a herd in the forest feeding on grasses and leaves. It makes a snorting sound as it moves quickly away from danger.

Giant Panda
The **giant panda** lives alone in the high, cold bamboo forests of Asia, feeding mainly on bamboo. Because of where it lives, it is difficult to study in the wild. This rare animal looks like a big white and black bear. It is shy and slow-moving and has a powerful jaw and huge teeth.

Gibbon
The **gibbon** is the smallest of the apes. This hairy animal has no tail and long, strong arms. It uses its long fingers like hooks. A **gibbon** lives in the treetops, usually eating fruit and leaves. It is known for making a very loud, shrieking noise.

Indian Elephant
The **Indian elephant** is usually gray and has much smaller ears and shorter tusks than the African elephant. It breathes and sucks water through its trunk. It lives in groups in forests and plains where it eats roots, leaves and fruit. It usually moves in a herd in single file.

Japanese Macaque
The **Japanese macaque** is also known as the **snow monkey.** Its long, shaggy gray-brown hair protects it from the cold. It spends most of its time on the ground but sleeps in the trees. These very social animals live in large groups and love to eat fruit, flowers and leaves.

King Cobra

The **king cobra** is the largest and most poisonous snake. It has the ability to move forward while standing on its tail. Its venom, or poison, can kill an animal within 20 minutes. The **king cobra** lives in forest areas and has been known to kill an animal as large as an elephant.

Loris

The **loris** is a slow-moving, furry creature with a pointed nose and large, round eyes. It rolls itself into a ball and sleeps in a hollow tree trunk during the day. At night, it hunts for lizards, insects and fruit. The **loris** can hang from a tree limb by its feet while eating fruit with its hands.

Lynx

The **lynx** is a short-tailed cat covered with spotted, thick fur. Its ears have tufts of black hair on them. The **lynx** lives alone in forests and rocky hillside areas. It hunts for rabbits, birds and small deer, mainly at night. It stalks its prey and then pounces on it.

Musk Deer

The male **musk deer** stores the world's most powerful perfume in a small pouch on its body. It is used in perfumes and soaps. Unlike other deer, it has no antlers. It has two inch tusk-like teeth which it uses to defend itself. The **musk deer** lives in the forest feeding on grass, bark and leaves.

Orangutan

This long-haired, orange ape lives on its own in the rain forest where it climbs and moves among the trees. It eats leaves, bark and flowers. The **orangutan** has very long arms and no tail. A baby lives with its mother for six to seven years until it is ready to take care of itself.

Proboscis Monkey

The most unusual feature of the **proboscis monkey** is its huge nose which may hang down over its mouth. This monkey lives in groups in the forest feeding on leaves and fruit. It can swim and dive very well but lives mostly in the trees.

Przewalski Wild Horse

The **przewalski wild horse** is reddish-brown with a dark brown mane that always stands up straight. It is the only wild horse left in the world. This stocky horse can go a long time without water and feeds on grass.

Saiga Antelope

The **saiga antelope** lives with 30 to 40 other antelopes. Its large head and nose gives it an unusual appearance. The male has light colored, long horns. It lives in muddy areas grazing on grasses. During the winter, it moves to warmer areas.

Siberian Tiger

The **siberian tiger** is the largest member of the cat family. This powerful animal has black or brown stripes on its long, thick coat. It usually hunts alone searching for deer, buffalo or other animals. The **siberian tiger** lives in the forest. There are fewer than 250 left in the world.

Snow Leopard

The **snow leopard's** long, thick fur is pale gray with large, rose-like spots on its coat. Its coloring helps it hide in its rocky surroundings. It is one of the most beautiful members of the cat family. This mountain animal hunts alone, mostly at night, searching for sheep, deer and other animals.

Water Buffalo

The **water buffalo** is gray or black and has the largest curved horns of any buffalo. It spends most of its time wallowing in the water or swimming. It rolls in mud to protect itself from insects. This bulky animal lives in a herd grazing on grasses.

Yak

This large, mountain animal has a long, woolly, dark colored coat to keep warm. Its curved horns grow from the sides of its head. Despite its size, it moves easily on rocks and climbs well. The **yak** eats grasses and plants and is easily tamed.

AUSTRALIA

Bilby
The **bilby** or rabbit-eared bandicoat is a small animal that is rare. During the day it sleeps in long burrows and comes out at night to hunt mice and insects. The **bilby** sniffs its surroundings with its long snout.

Dingo
The **dingo** is the wild dog of Australia. Yellow-brown fur covers its body. It usually lives alone or in pairs and inhabits semi-desert areas. Rabbits and small kangaroos are its main prey.

Duck-billed Platypus

This strange-looking animal has a bill and webbed feet like a duck, fur like an otter and a tail like a beaver. It is an egg-laying mammal that lives in mud-bottomed streams. The **platypus** eats half its weight in food each day feasting on shrimp and worms. The male has poisonous spurs on its hind feet which it uses to protect itself.

Echidna

The **echidna** or **spiney anteater** is an unusual mammal because it lays eggs. After the egg hatches, the young **echidna** is carried in the mother's pouch for about eight weeks. The **echidna** is covered with spines and has a long, tube-shaped snout. It eats ants with its long, sticky tongue and rolls itself into a ball when attacked.

Frilled Lizard

The **frilled lizard** is a scary-looking creature. It frightens its enemies by opening its mouth and making a hissing noise. When it does this, it unfolds the large frill that goes around its head. It raises the front of its body to run on its hind legs. Its long tail helps keep its balance.

Greater Glider

The **greater glider** moves about at night. It pushes off from a tree branch launching its body into the air. Flaps of skin catch the air as it glides to another tree. This furry, possum-like animal eats leaves, fruit and insects.

Koala

The **koala** looks like a cuddly teddy bear but it is not a bear at all. The cub rides in its mother's pouch for six months after it is born. Then it rides on the mother's back or follows close by until it is old enough to be on its own. **Koalas** live in the treetops feeding only on the leaves of eucalyptus trees.

Numbat

This small, hairy mammal with a long, pointed snout lives in wooded areas. A **numbat** lives on termites it collects with its long, sticky tongue. It likes to lay in the sun in the winter.

Red Kangaroo

The **red kangaroo** lives in the dry desert and plains of Australia. It gets from place to place by jumping. It can leap almost 30 feet in one jump. A young **kangaroo**, called a joey, spends its first six months growing in its mother's pouch. This furry marsupial, or animal with a pouch, likes to live in groups.

Spotted Cuscus

This marsupial, an animal that carries its baby in its pouch, is about the size of a cat. It lives in the treetops feeding on leaves, fruit and insects. It uses the tip of its tail as an extra hand. The **spotted cuscus** has a woolly, grey coat with white spots, big yellow eyes and a yellow nose.

Tasmanian Devil

The **tasmanian devil** is about the size of a small dog. It has a very powerful jaw which it uses to catch and eat its prey. It is slow moving but strong and clever so it catches its prey by surprise.

Thorny Devil

The **thorny devil** is a horned lizard. It looks scary but is harmless. This reptile lives in the sandy desert and eats ants one at a time. It is too slow to escape its enemies but it protects itself by being covered with spines.

Wallaroo

A **wallaroo** is a furry member of the kangaroo family. It is stocky with short hind legs and a long tail which it uses as a third leg. **Wallaroos** are not very active and can live without water for long periods of time.

Wombat

The **wombat** waddles on short, powerful legs. It uses its front paws to dig tunnels. It sleeps in the tunnel during the day and comes out at night to feed on grass and roots. This hairy animal runs back into the ground when it senses danger.

EUROPE

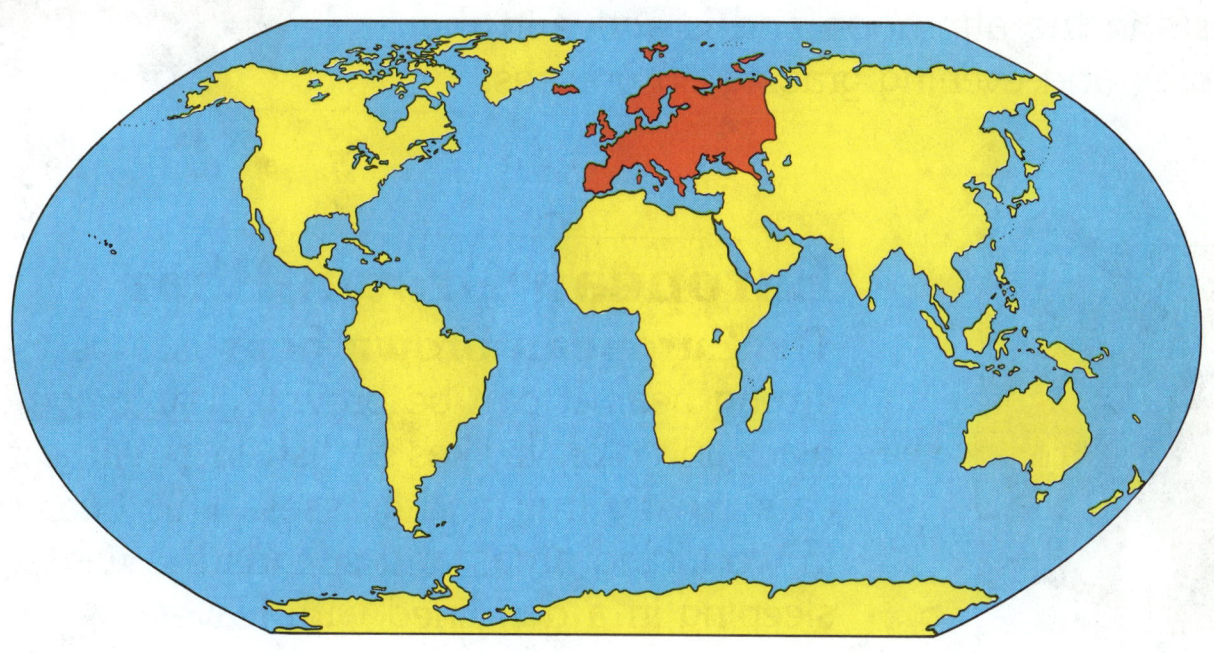

Chamois
The **chamois** grows a new set of rings on each of its black horns every summer. It has a great sense of balance and can leap high in the air. It lives high in the mountains grazing on herbs, flowers and grass. A **chamois** will whistle to other members of its herd and stamp its hooves to signal danger.

Eurasian Badger
The **Eurasian badger** is a playful animal that becomes vicious when attacked. There are black stripes on its white head. It lives in groups called "clans" in wooded areas and hunts for animals, fruit and plants at night. It spends the day and winter in underground tunnels.

European Bison

The **European bison** is a huge animal with a long, thick coat. It has two horns that curve upward from the side of its head. The **European bison** lives in the forest in herds. It rests in the afternoon and is active in the morning and evening grazing on grasses.

European Brown Bear

The **European brown bear** is a very large, strong bear. It can be brown, gray, beige or black in color. It likes to fish in streams and eats mostly fruit and grasses. This bear lives in woodland areas and spends the winter sleeping in a den lined with leaves.

European Mole

The **European mole** is a small creature with very large hands sticking out from its body. It uses these hands as shovels to dig underground tunnels. The **mole** lives in these tunnels and eats mainly worms found in the soil. It has very tiny eyes hidden by fur and can barely see.

Fallow Deer

The **fallow deer** is a graceful animal with a reddish coat with white speckles. Male deer grow antlers which they shed annually. The antlers are shaped like a hand with fingers at the tip. It lives in rocky areas and forests, and eats grass, bark and leaves.

Ferret

The **ferret** is a small, furry animal that lives in forests and grasslands. It has a long neck and usually has pink eyes. It eats mice, rabbits and squirrels. If it kills more than it can eat, it stores the rest in its underground burrow. It sleeps in this burrow during the day.

Gray Seal

The **gray seal** lives in the coastal waters of the North Atlantic Ocean. Its thick neck has three folds of skin and it has curved claws on its front flippers. Its coat looks black when it is wet. The **gray seal** lives in groups. These groups of seals feed together on many types of fish.

Hedgehog

The **hedgehog** is protected by spiny armor. When it rolls itself in a ball, it looks like a pin cushion with thousands of needles sticking out. Each night it looks for insects, mice and birds to eat. The **hedgehog** can live almost anywhere. When it is angry it screams, coughs and wheezes.

Ibex

The **ibex** is a kind of wild goat with a short, brown coat. It has two heavy, ridged horns on its head that keep growing year after year. The **ibex** lives in mountainous and rocky regions and can balance easily on the edge of cliffs. It grazes on grass, herbs and plants.

Mouflon

The **mouflon** is a brown, wild sheep with thick, white horns on its head that turn downward. It is one of the smallest of the wild sheep and lives in forest areas and low mountainous regions. The **mouflon** grazes on grasses and can move very quickly from place to place.

Raccoon Dog

The **raccoon dog** is a wild dog that gets its name from the raccoon-like mask on its face. Its dark brown fur grows thicker and longer in the winter to keep it warm. It hunts for food at night, eating small animals, insects, fruit and nuts. The **raccoon dog** lives alone in the forest.

Wild Boar

The **wild boar** has a stiff, bristly coat of brownish hair. It has a pig-like snout and two curved tusks. Often wild boars live in groups of 20 to 30 in woodland areas. It is a very powerful, aggressive animal which feeds on mostly vegetables and berries.

Wolverine

The **wolverine** is a furry animal that looks like a bear with a short bushy tail. It has great strength and a keen sense of smell. It roams woodland areas by itself constantly searching for food. The **wolverine** eats many different kinds of food including animals, berries, eggs and plants.

NORTH AMERICA

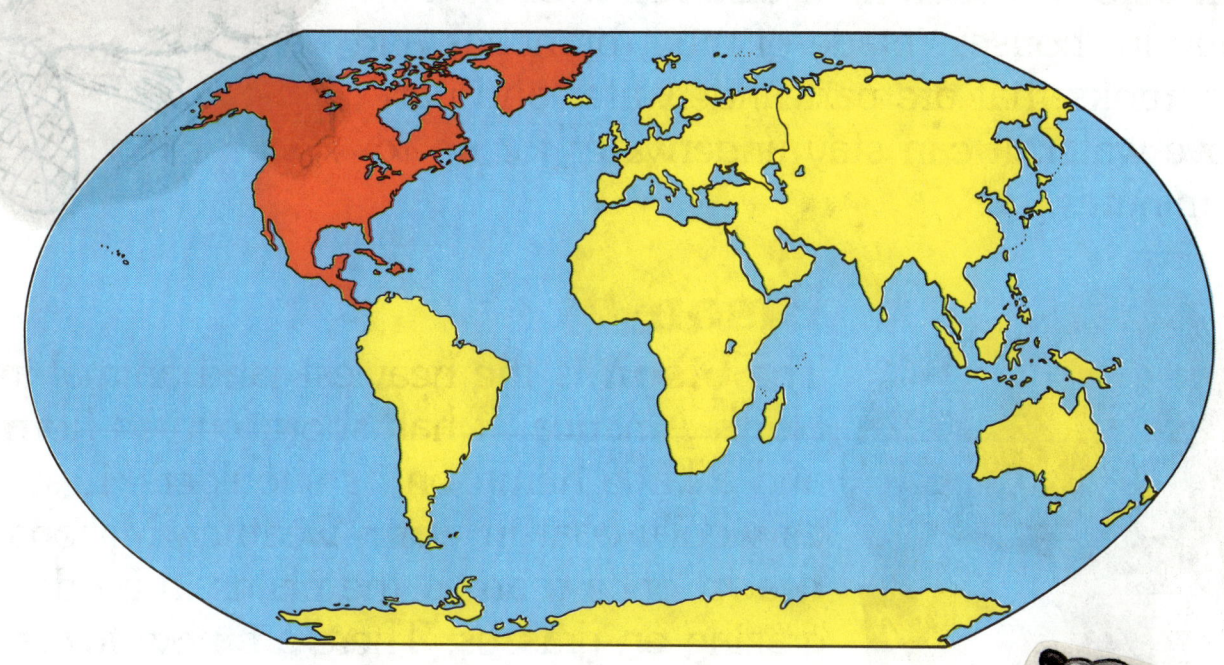

American Black Bear
The **American black bear** is the best known bear in America. Its coat can be other colors besides black. This meat-eating bear is usually active at night and will eat almost anything. It is an excellent swimmer and tree climber and lives mostly in woodland areas.

Bald Eagle

The **bald eagle** is the national symbol of the United States and lives only in North America. It has white feathers on its neck and head that make it appear bald. This beautiful bird has keen eyesight, powerful wings and great strength. It captures fish, birds and small animals for food.

Beaver

The **beaver** lives in rivers, lakes and streams. It can cut down a tree with its large, powerful teeth. It uses the wood to build a dam across a stream. A **beaver** lives in a group in "houses" made of mud, branches and tree trunks that are part underwater and part above water. It can stay underwater for up to 15 minutes.

Bison

The **bison** is the heaviest land animal in North America. It has short, curved horns and a large hump on its shoulders. It sheds its woolly coat in warm weather. Millions of **bison** once roamed the plains in herds grazing on grasses. There are now fewer than 35,000 living in protected areas.

Black-tailed Prairie Dog

The **black-tailed prairie dog** is a large ground squirrel. It lives with many others in underground "towns" connected by big tunnels. It comes out of its burrow to feed on grasses and insects. A **prairie dog** is very vocal and has nine different calls, each with a different meaning.

Bobcat

The **bobcat** has soft, tan fur spotted with white, gray or black. This shy, strong animal can leap 10 feet to catch an animal to eat. It usually lives alone among rocks, in bushes and in caves. It gets its name from its short, stubby tail which looks cut off, or "bobbed".

Coyote

The **coyote** lives on the plains, in the desert, forests and mountains. It is a very clever animal that will prey on almost anything. It lives in a family group and fiercely protects its area. In the evening, it "sings" by yelping, barking and howling loudly.

Eastern Diamondback Rattlesnake

The **eastern diamondback rattlesnake** is the largest poisonous rattlesnake in the United States. Its back has a dark, diamond-shaped pattern on it. When disturbed, it stands still, lifts its head and rattles the coil at the end of its tail as a warning. It lives in dry woodlands where it eats rodents.

Grizzly Bear

A **grizzly bear** is a bear with thick, brown fur that is "grizzled" or streaked with a lighter color. This very large bear has a keen sense of smell and can be dangerous. It lives in the mountains eating almost anything it can find. When it hibernates, or sleeps for the winter, it often awakens and leaves its den.

Mink

The **mink** is prized for its beautiful brown or black coat. In the wild, it lives alone near rivers, lakes and ponds feeding on small animals. The **mink** is usually active at night and is an excellent climber and able swimmer.

Moose

The **moose** is the largest living deer. It has a big head and a flattened mouth. An adult male develops huge antlers which may grow to over six feet. It sheds these antlers every year and grows a new pair. A **moose** lives in the forest and stays mainly in the water or mud feeding on plants.

Mountain Goat

Thick, white woolly hair keeps the **mountain goat** protected from wind, rain and snow. It lives in the snowy regions of the Rocky Mountains. You can tell the age of a **mountain goat** by counting the rings on its black horns. It lives alone or in a small flock and grazes on plants and tree bark.

Porcupine

A prickly coat of sharp quills covers the **porcupine's** body. There are 30,000 quills on its back, sides and tail. If an enemy comes too close, it raises and spreads its quills to protect itself. Active at night in wooded areas, it looks for leaves and tree bark to eat.

Pronghorn

The **pronghorn** is an antelope that sheds the outer sheath of its branched horns once a year. It has a brown coat with white markings on its face and body. Because its eyes are on the side of its head, it can watch for enemies in most directions. The **pronghorn** lives in herds in grassland areas feeding on plants.

Raccoon

The **raccoon's** black-masked face and bushy, ringed tail can be found in the city and in the wilderness. It is a playful animal, a skilled climber and an excellent swimmer. A **raccoon** will eat almost anything, finding food wherever it can. It has skilled front paws that can explore and feel around for food.

Red Fox

The **red fox** is a shy, nervous animal that hunts mostly at night for small animals. It also eats vegetables, apples, corn and cherries. The **red fox** uses its long, furry tail to cover its feet and nose in the winter. It also uses it to help keep its balance. It rests and sleeps in a den or small cave.

Snowshoe Hare

This furry, long-eared animal is one of the smallest hares. In the summer, its fur is brown with white underneath and in winter it turns white. It has very large hind feet that look like big snowshoes. At night, the **snowshoe hare** feeds on grasses and berries and spends its days resting in protected areas.

White-Tailed Deer

The **white-tailed deer** is the most common of the country's large mammals. Males have antlers sprouting from their heads. They shed them once a year. A young deer stays with its mother one or two years. The **white-tailed deer** eats a variety of plants. It is a strong swimmer and a good runner.

SOUTH AMERICA

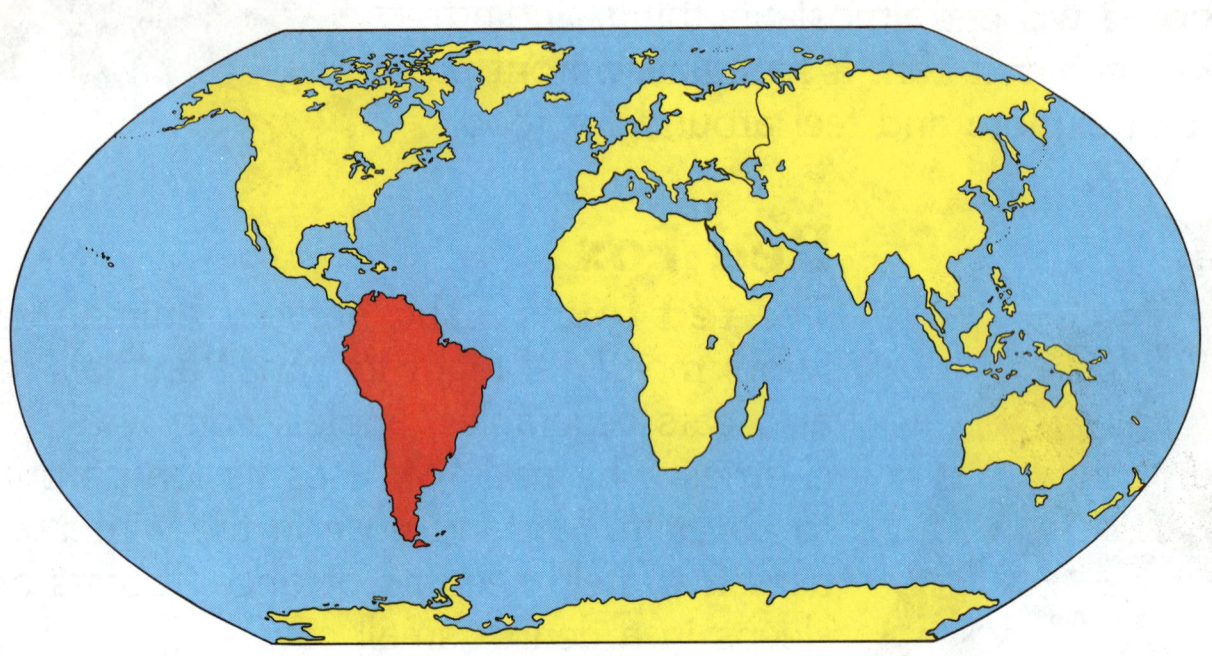

Alpaca
The **alpaca** is related to the camel and looks like a llama. It is raised for its fine woolly coat which is used to make cloth. The **alpaca** lives high in the Andes Mountains where it grazes on grasses and other plants.

Chinchilla
The **chinchilla** is a small animal that looks like a furry squirrel. It has soft, silver-gray hair and has been hunted for its beautiful fur. Most **chinchillas** are raised on farms. In the wild, the **chinchilla** lives in the Andes Mountains where it eats roots and grasses.

Coati

The **coati** is a member of the raccoon family with a long, ringed tail that stands straight up. The **coati's** fur can be sandy-colored to dark brown. Its long, sharp claws dig up insects and small animals for it to eat. It lives in trees and on the ground in wooded areas.

Condor

The **South American condor** is a giant vulture. It lives high in the Andes Mountains and feeds mainly on the bodies of dead animals. It nests in caves high on cliffs. The **condor** has a large wingspan and may fly as high as 20,000 feet.

Giant Anteater

The **giant anteater** has a long, narrow head and tube-shaped snout. It has no teeth, but has a long, sticky tongue which it uses to lick up ants and termites. A **giant anteater** can grow to over six feet long and can weigh as much as 75 pounds.

Giant Armadillo

The **giant armadillo's** shell is its best protection. The animal is covered with hard, bony plates and uses its strong claws to dig tunnels. When it senses danger, it hurries into a tunnel or hides in its shell. It licks up insects with its long tongue.

Giant Otter

The **giant otter** can grow to seven feet long. It is an excellent swimmer and spends much of its time in rivers and streams. It can close its ears and nostrils for many minutes so it can stay underwater to catch fish to eat. An **otter** is a very playful animal that loves to play with other **otters.**

Jaguar

The **jaguar** is the most powerful and largest wildcat found in Central and South America. It hides in forests and grasslands and hunts other animals for food. A **jaguar** usually has yellowish fur covered with dark spots, but some are all black.

Llama

The **llama** is a member of the camel family but has no hump. Its hair is thick and long and may be brown, gray, white or black. A **llama** can live without water for many weeks. It gets moisture from the plants it eats. If it is angry, it spits in its enemy's face.

Marmoset

The **marmoset** is one of the world's smallest monkeys. Most weigh less than one pound. Thick, soft, golden hair covers its entire body. During the day, a **marmoset** travels in a family group scampering from tree to tree. It eats insects and fruit.

Mountain Lion
The powerful **mountain lion** is a large wildcat. It can be many different colors and has long legs and a slender body. It lives in the forests where it travels long distances hunting for animals to eat. The **mountain lion's** cry can be very scary.

Ocelot
The **ocelot** is a spotted member of the cat family. It has stripes on its face and forelegs. During the day it sleeps and at night it hunts for animals and birds to eat. An **ocelot** lives in many types of areas. It is a skilled climber but lives on the ground most of the time.

Opossum
The **opossum** is a furry animal that carries its young in a pouch for about 2 months. An **opossum** hunts for food at night eating animals and vegetables. If it senses danger it lies very still and plays dead. This is known as "playing possum."

Sloth
The **sloth** is a very slow moving animal. It looks very unusual because it has almost no tail or ears. Its teeth are peglike. The **sloth** lives mostly in the trees and walks upside-down when it moves from branch to branch. It sleeps during the day and searches for leaves to eat at night.

Spider Monkey

The **spider monkey** uses its tail to pick up things. It can hang by its tail upside down from a tree branch. When it does this, it looks like a spider. The **spider monkey** lives and plays in the branches with many other monkeys and collects fruit and nuts to eat.

Tapir

The **tapir** is a short-haired animal that looks much like a pig. It has a long nose and an excellent sense of smell. The **tapir** lives in forests and near water. It loves to swim. It feeds on fruits and vegetables.

Vampire Bat

The **vampire bat** is a scary-looking, little creature. It is about three inches long and is reddish-brown in color. It cannot swallow pieces of food so it feeds only on liquids. The **vampire bat** attacks animals to drink their blood.

Vicuña

The **vicuña** is the smallest member of the camel family. However, it has no hump. Its long, woolly, beautiful coat is cut and used to make wool cloth. The **vicuña** has excellent eyesight and can run very swiftly from danger. It feeds on grasses.